C0-AJY-887

Newfoundland and Labrador

Harry Beckett

Weigl

Published by Weigl Educational Publishers Limited
6325 – 10 Street SE
Calgary, Alberta, Canada
T2H 2Z9

Website: www.weigl.ca

Library and Archives Canada Cataloguing in Publication
Beckett, Harry, 1936-, author
Newfoundland and Labrador / Harry Beckett.
(Provinces)
Issued in print and electronic formats.
ISBN 978-1-4872-0260-6 (bound).--ISBN 978-1-4872-0261-3 (pbk.).--
ISBN 978-1-4872-0262-0 (ebook)
1. Newfoundland and Labrador--Juvenile literature. I. Title.
FC2161.2.B433 2015 j971.8 C2015-900979-0
C2015-900980-4

Printed in the United States of America in Brainerd, Minnesota
1 2 3 4 5 6 7 8 9 0 19 18 17 16 15

082015
100815

We acknowledge the financial support of the Government of Canada through the Canada Book Fund for our publishing activities.

Photograph Credits
Every reasonable effort has been made to trace ownership and to obtain permission to reprint copyright material. The publishers would be pleased to have any errors or omissions brought to their attention so that they may be corrected in subsequent printings.

Weigl acknowledges Getty Images, Corbis Images, Alamy, And Newscom as the primary image suppliers for this title.

Project Coordinator: Heather Kissock
Designer: Terry Paulhus

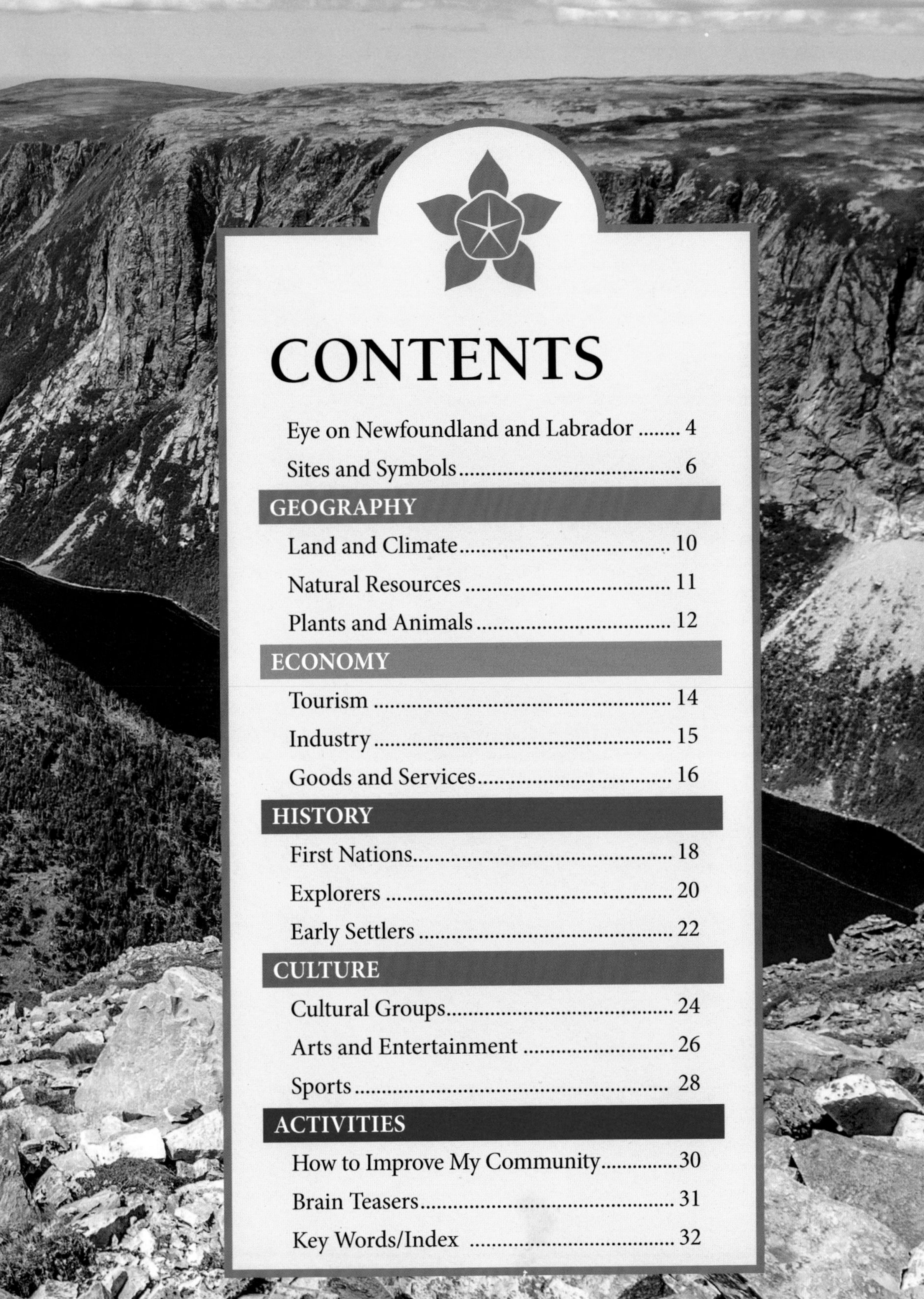

CONTENTS

Eye on Newfoundland and Labrador

Newfoundland, properly called Newfoundland and Labrador, is the easternmost province of Canada. It has two separate land masses—Newfoundland, which is an island, and Labrador, which is part of the Canadian mainland. Both the island and Labrador have long, rugged coastlines. Labrador has Quebec on all its borders but the east, where it looks out on the Atlantic Ocean.

Newfoundland and Labrador are unique in appearance. During the Ice Age, glaciers thousands of metres thick covered the province. They scraped the soil off the rock below, deepened the river valleys, and rounded the mountains. When the glaciers retreated, they left hollows dug out by the ice. Thousands of shallow lakes and **bogs** were left in these hollows. The largest lakes on the island are the Gander, the Red Indian, and the Grand.

Ancient Newfoundland

Newfoundland is Canada's youngest province, but it is one of the oldest settled regions in North America. Archaeologists and scholars have dated a site in Labrador to 5500 BC, and remains at Port aux Choix indicate that people lived there as early as 2340 BC. **Excavations** have also revealed that Vikings settled along Newfoundland's coastline in the year 1000 AD.

Gros Morne National Park, located on Newfoundland's west coast, is home to an array of plants and animals. Jellyfish are just one of the creatures found in the surrounding waters.

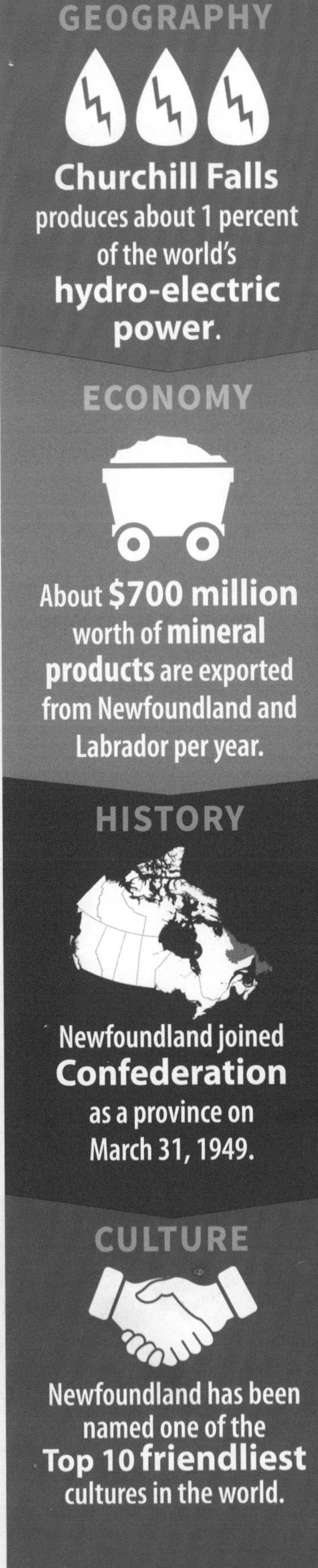

Sites and Symbols

Entered Confederation: March 31, 1949

Capital: St. John's

Area: 405,212 sq. km

Population: 514,536

Newfoundland and Labrador has its own unique identity. It uses a variety of symbols to represent this identity to Canada and the world. These symbols showcase the people, history, culture, and natural beauty of the province.

What's in a Name?

Newfoundland and Labrador were named separately. As the island was one of the first areas in North America explored by Europeans, explorer John Cabot called it the "new founde isle." In official documents, this became "New found launde," which finally developed into Newfoundland. Labrador's name comes from the Portuguese word *lavrador*, which means "landholder." This name came from João Fernandes, a Portuguese landholder who explored the area.

The Newfoundland and Labrador Confederation Centre stands in St. John's. The Centre is the seat of legislature for the province.

The Provincial Coat of Arms

The coat of arms of Newfoundland and Labrador is made up of the shield, its supporters, and the motto. The shield is split into four parts by St. John's Cross, in honour of the discovery of Newfoundland on the feast of St. John. There are two lions and two unicorns on the shield. On the sides, two Beothuk warriors support the shield. They were an Aboriginal group in Newfoundland. On the bottom of the coat of arms is the Latin motto, *Quaerite Prime Regnum Dei.* It means "Seek Ye First the Kingdom of God."

Newfoundland and Labrador's Official Flag

Newfoundland and Labrador adopted its flag in 1980. The flag uses colours for symbolism. White represents snow and ice, blue represents the sea, red represents human effort, and gold represents confidence in the future. The right half of the flag looks like a trident, which honours the importance of fishing and the sea.

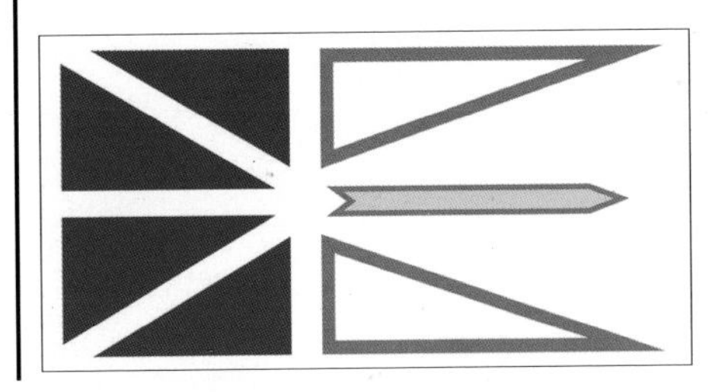

Newfoundland and Labrador Map

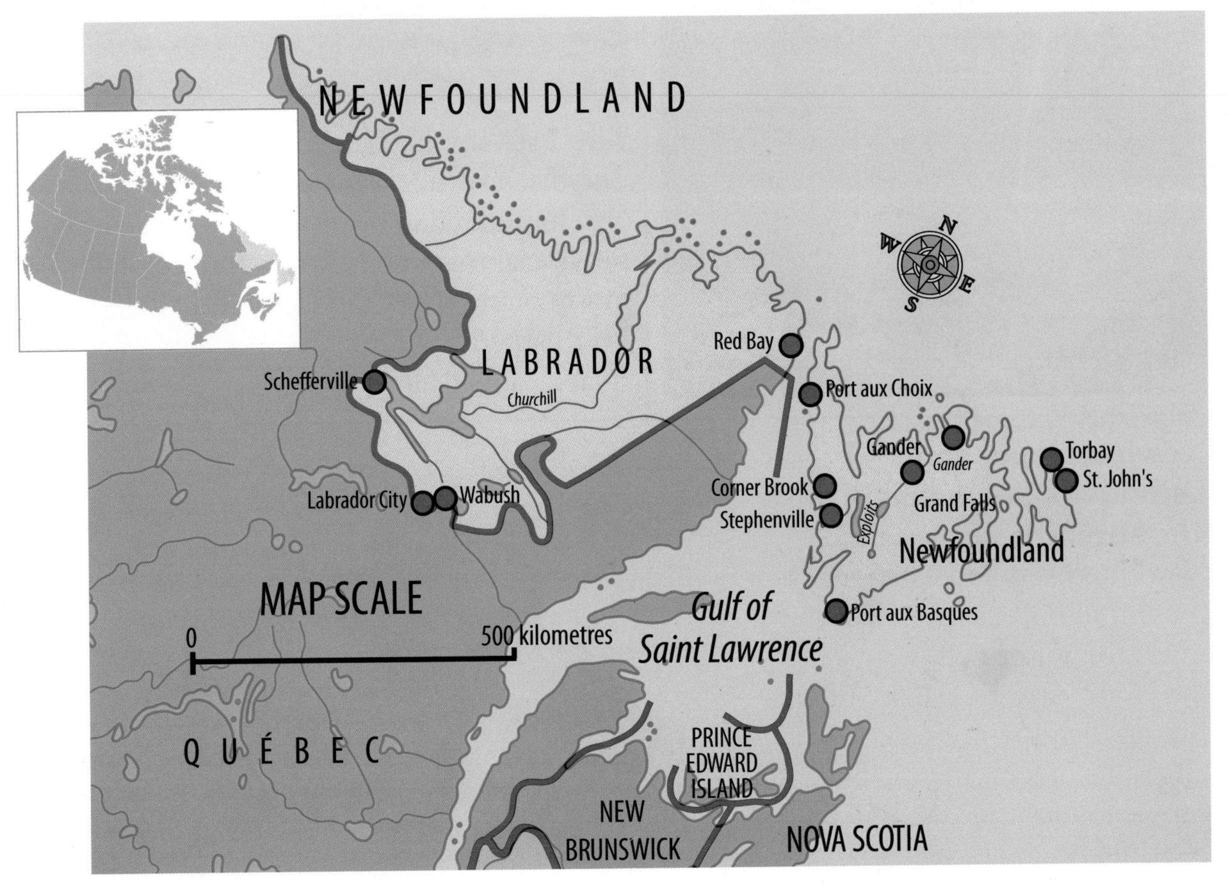

Newfoundland and Labrador's Flower Emblem

The pitcher plant officially became Newfoundland and Labrador's flower emblem in 1954. It grows in the wetlands, marshes, and bogs of the province. Queen Victoria originally suggested the plant as a symbol of Newfoundland. Its picture was printed on the island's coins. The pitcher plant eats insects and soaks up their nutrients.

The Provincial Tree

The black spruce was named Newfoundland and Labrador's provincial tree in 1993. It is the region's most common tree, and is found all over Labrador. Although it is called "black," it is really a bluish-green colour.

Newfoundland and Labrador's Provincial Bird

The Atlantic puffin became Newfoundland and Labrador's provincial bird in 1991. This bird lives around the cold waters of the North Atlantic. Most puffins live on the province's coast. The largest colony of Atlantic puffins can be found near the capital of St. John's.

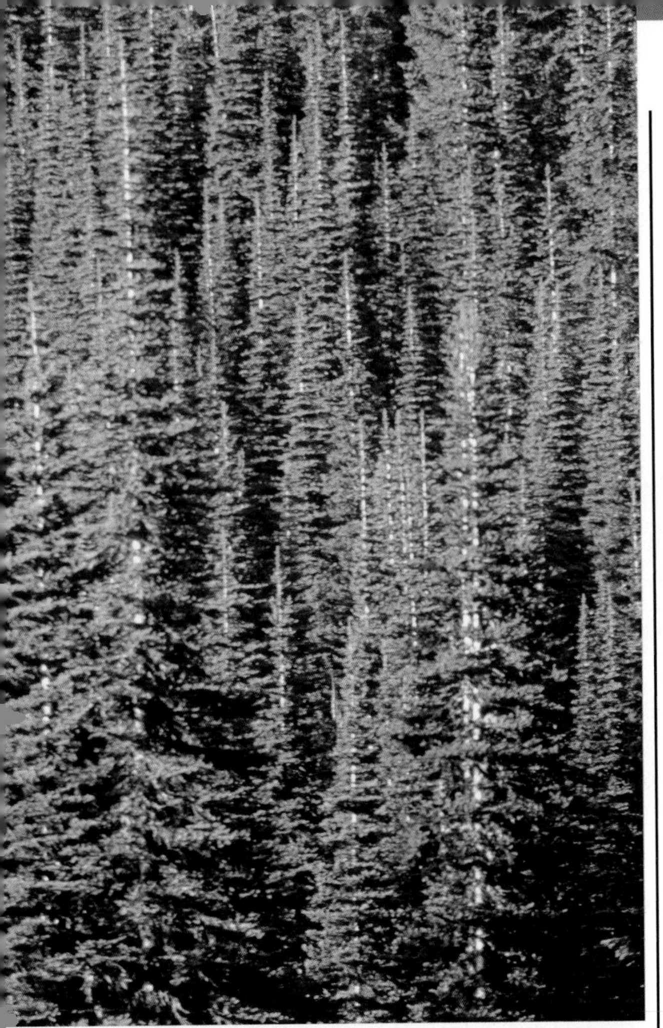

The Provincial Animal

Newfoundland and Labrador has two provincial animals, the Newfoundland dog and the Newfoundland pony. The Newfoundland dog was originally bred to be a working dog to help fishers and forest workers. The Newfoundland pony was bred from the ponies that early European settlers brought to the province.

Newfoundland and Labrador's Official Mineral

Labradorite is Newfoundland and Labrador's provincial gemstone. It was chosen because of the many **deposits** of the gem in the province. Labradorite reflects light in a special way, revealing beautiful colours. The Beothuk called it "firestone" because of this property.

The Official Game Bird

Newfoundland and Labrador's official game bird is the partridge. There are two different partridge species that live in the province. This arctic bird is mainly found in the wilderness areas.

Deep fjords slice through the Torngat Mountains, some reaching far into the interior of the range.

LAND AND CLIMATE

Newfoundland is made up of two regions—the Appalachian Region and the **Canadian Shield**. Southeastern Labrador and all of the island are part of the Appalachian Region. This land is mostly a **plateau** with parts that rise up to 610 metres high. There are also rugged hills, bogs, and small lakes in the flat, rolling plateaus of the south and east. North-central Newfoundland island is fairly flat, with gently rolling hills.

The **highest** temperature ever recorded in Newfoundland was **36.7 ° C,** in 1976.

Most of Labrador is made up of the rocky plateaus of the Canadian Shield. It is a land of **tundra**, ice, and barren rock. In Northern Labrador, the Torngat Mountains dot the land. The highest point in Newfoundland is Mount Caubvick. It stands 1,622 metres above sea level.

Northern Labrador is a subarctic region—it has cool summers and cold winters. Average July temperatures reach only to about 13° Celsius, but they also drop as low as –51°C. In January, the temperature usually sits at about –18°C. The island's temperature is much more pleasant. July temperatures average 15°C, and January temperatures drop to about –4°C. However, winter temperatures can reach –34°C throughout the season.

Iron-ore, nickel, copper, zinc, cobalt, and gold come from Newfoundland's seven metal mines.

NATURAL RESOURCES

Newfoundland and Labrador have many mineral resources. Silver, gold, and nickel are a few of the many minerals hidden in the Canadian Shield of Labrador. Labrador also has rich deposits of iron-ore, which account for a large portion of Newfoundland's mineral income. In 1994, large deposits of nickel, copper, and cobalt were found at Voisey's Bay. Gypsum, asbestos, and limestone are also mined on the island.

Among other important minerals in the province are the deposits of oil and natural gas that lie in the coastal waters. In 1959, engineers discovered the Hibernia fields off Newfoundland's coast. Huge petroleum deposits were found in this region.

In the past, Newfoundland and Labrador also depended on another important natural resource, fish. Workers fished along the coast as part of a large industry. Today, the fishing industry is still worth about $1 billion, but it has slowed down because of over-fishing. The province now depends more on minerals and lumber.

PLANTS AND ANIMALS

Forests, mostly in the river valley, cover about one third of Newfoundland. White and black spruce, balsam fir, birch, and aspen trees grow in the province. Smaller plants, such as sheep laurel, blueberry, pigeonberry, and snakeberry, grow on the forest floor. Labrador tea, sundews, and pitcher plants flourish in marshy areas.

Some of Labrador's trees must struggle to grow in the poor soil and harsh climate. The ground is covered with common juniper, dwarf willow, and ground laurel. Reindeer moss and lichens are common in the barren lands. Only mosses and some low bushes can survive in the harsh northern tundra.

Woodland caribou and black bears, as well as small mammals such as otters, beavers, muskrats, foxes, and lynxes, are found throughout the province. Wolves, porcupines, martens, and huge herds of caribou call Labrador home. Polar bears are native to the north coast.

The sundew, like the pitcher plant, eats insects.

Off the east coast, where the cold Labrador current mixes with the warm Gulf Stream, conditions are ideal for seals, whales, porpoises, dolphins, and many fish species. To preserve fish stocks, the federal government banned fishing for northern cod and other species in 1992. Their numbers were low, most likely from over-fishing by people and by the seal population.

Three hundred different species of birds nest on the Newfoundland shore. Many kinds of ducks and geese live in the province during the summer. Millions of gulls, gannets, murres, kittiwakes, and puffins nest around the coasts. Sanctuaries have been set up to protect them.

Newfoundland and Labrador's Greenland seal population migrates around the province.

Canada lynxes can be found in forested areas of Newfoundland and Labrador, where they prey mainly on snowshoe hare.

Visitors to Signal Hill National Historic Site climb to the top of the hill to see the sights from Cabot Tower.

TOURISM

Tourism is a rapidly growing industry in Newfoundland. Visitors come from all over the world to see the province's rugged beauty and fascinating history.

St. John's is the oldest North American city north of Mexico. At St. John's Signal Hill National Historic Site, visitors are treated to a wonderful view of the town, the coast, and the port. For tourists interested in history, the Queen's Battery is a popular attraction. It is a fort from the time of the Napoleonic Wars. Today, actors re-enact the English and French battles of the 1800s.

22 species of **whales** can be spotted in the waters around Newfoundland and Labrador.

The Newfoundland Museum is also in St. John's. There, visitors get the chance to learn more about the province's history. Some exhibits are devoted to the lives of its Aboriginal Peoples, while others demonstrate the lifestyles of nineteenth-century settlers. Many tourists head to the northern tip of Newfoundland to explore the L'Anse aux Meadows National Historic Site. The Viking settlement at L'Anse aux Meadows dates back to the year 1000, and is the only known Viking settlement in North America. Visitors can walk among the reconstructed sod houses and learn how they were built.

Tourists can view icebergs by boat or kayak, or on land.

INDUSTRY

Newfoundland and Labrador's economy is quite dependent on natural resources. One of Newfoundland's most important industries is fishing. Salmon, turbot, halibut, and flounder swim in the coastal waters. A ban on cod fishing in 1992 hit many fishing communities hard, but it also helped rebuild the stocks. Limited cod fishing is now allowed. In 2013, more than 26,000 tonnes of fish were caught in Newfoundland and Labrador.

The forestry industry in Newfoundland and Labrador makes up $250 million of the local economy.

Forestry and mining are other important industries in the province. About two-thirds of Newfoundland's harvested wood is used to make newsprint. Newfoundland wood is also made into lumber and timber products.

Labrador's vast resources of iron ore are a major part of the province's mining industry. Iron ore mining accounts for about 90 percent of the province's mining income. About one half of the nation's supply comes from Labrador.

Hydro-electric power is a critical product. Newfoundland's Churchill Falls has 11 generators that use the power of falling water to produce electricity. People in Newfoundland only need about 29 percent of the total electricity generated by the falls. The rest is exported, mostly to Quebec.

Herring are one of the many fish caught off the coast of Newfoundland.

Most of the grain grown in Newfoundland and Labrador is used as feed for the dairy sector.

GOODS AND SERVICES

Newfoundland's economy relies heavily on farm products. Agricultural goods bring in about $75 million each year. Since the province has a difficult climate and uncooperative soil, farmers must grow crops that will survive under poor conditions. Potatoes, turnips, cabbage, carrots, and beets are the most important vegetable crops produced in the province. Farmers have expanded their scope to include broccoli, cauliflower, and lettuce. Wild blueberries are abundant, and are exported to other provinces.

Dairy products make up about one-third of the province's total agricultural industry. Newfoundland exports milk to other provinces, and the dairy industry creates about $27 million for the economy. Dairy cows and chickens are the most important animals in the province. Other livestock in Newfoundland include goats, beef cattle, and pigs. Animal farming provides hundreds of jobs both on farms and in processing and distribution.

Newfoundland's main manufactured goods include processed fish and newsprint. Manufacturing in the province has had to overcome the small market size, the distance to other markets, and the shortage

Dairy farmers in Newfoundland and Labrador produce more than 48 million litres of milk per year.

of skilled workers. Most factories in Newfoundland are located around St. John's. These factories manufacture goods such as food, paint, and fishing equipment. There are also small sawmills, seafood canneries, and brickyards.

About three-quarters of Newfoundland's employees work in the service industry. Service jobs include those in hotels and restaurants, airports, transportation, and government. Doctors are also in the service industry. Most health services in the province are free, and the province is combining hospitals to provide better service and economy.

The health care industry has some of the highest-paid employees in Newfoundland and Labrador.

FIRST NATIONS

When the first Europeans arrived, there were a number of Aboriginal groups living throughout the Labrador and Newfoundland regions. A group called the Innu lived in central Labrador and on parts of the Labrador coast. The Innu were nomadic hunters of large animals such as caribou. North of the Innu lived the Inuit. Like the Innu, the Inuit hunted caribou and moved from camp to camp. The Inuit are distantly related to the Dorset. The Dorset lived in Newfoundland from 500 BC to 1500 AD. They hunted sea mammals such as arctic whales and walruses.

It is commonly believed that the Beothuk were the first Aboriginal Peoples encountered by Viking explorers when they arrived on the island of Newfoundland. The Beothuk lived in small, conical **wigwams** in the summer. They hunted, fished, and collected eggs and shellfish. In winter, they lived in large log structures lined with moss to keep out the cold.

Inuit elders show younger generations how to make traditional items, such as sealskin kamiks. Kamiks are boots that protect the feet from extreme cold conditions.

The last known **Beothuk**, Shanawdithit, died in 1829.

During the spring and fall migrations, the Beothuk forced caribou, their main meat source, to cross rivers at certain points and hunted them from their canoes.

When the Mi'kmaq migrated to Newfoundland from Nova Scotia, they lived peacefully with the Beothuk until around 1770. Then, other settlers encouraged the Mi'kmaq to attack the Beothuk. It was these attacks, along with the arrival of more European settlers and diseases, that led the Beothuk to eventually die out.

The Innu still practise their traditional ways of life through hunting, fishing, and food gathering.

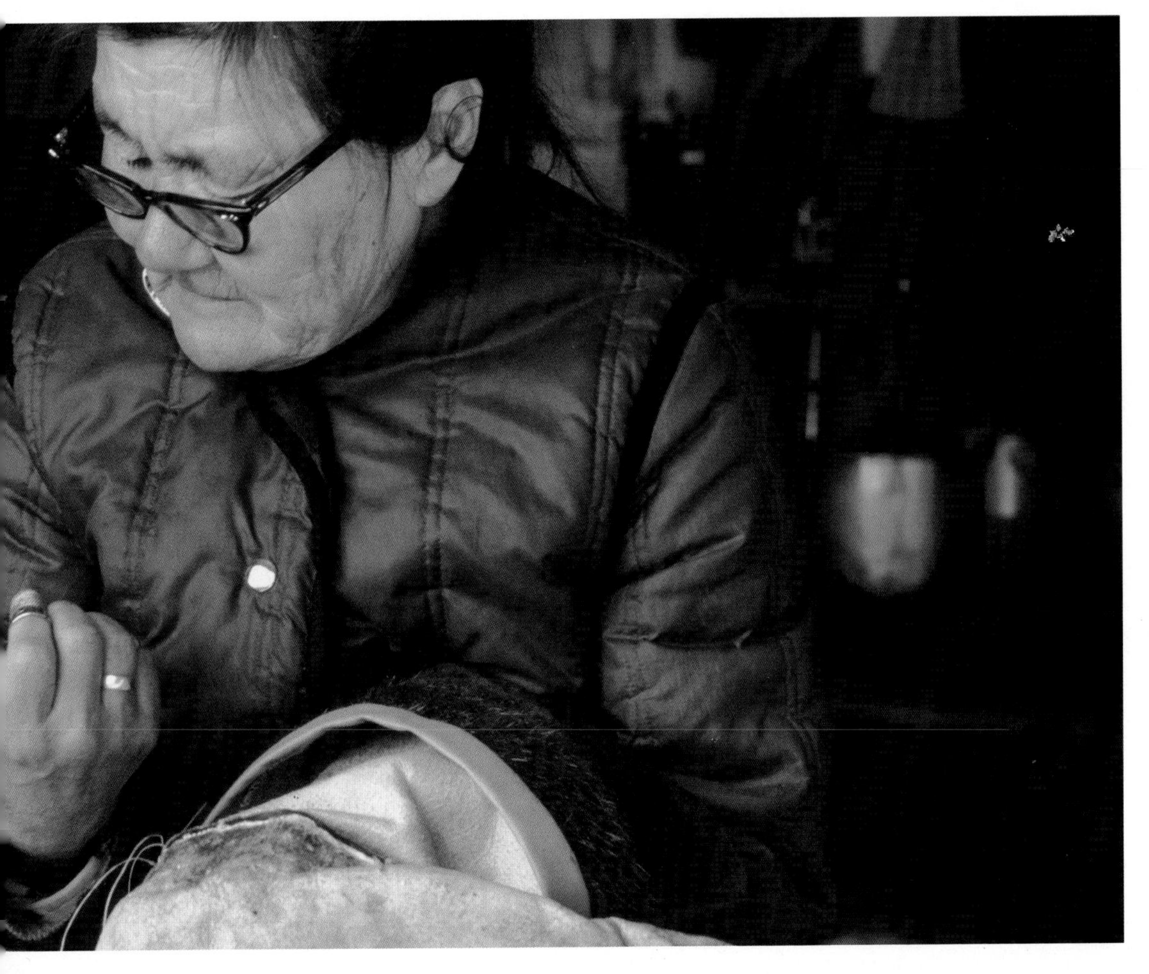

EXPLORERS

Vikings were likely the first Europeans to explore the shores of Newfoundland. In 986 AD, the European Bjarni Herjolfssom described the coast of Labrador in his descriptions of North America. Around the year 1000, Norse explorer Leif Ericson made several voyages west and southwest from Greenland. The discovery of nine Viking buildings near L'Anse aux Meadows shows that either Ericson or some other Norse explorer established a temporary settlement there. The Vikings may have stayed in the area for about 20 years, but abandoned it after attacks by local Aboriginal Peoples.

Five hundred years later, Portuguese and English explorers looking for the **Northwest Passage** to the Orient probably touched on the Newfoundland coast. In 1497, a navigator called John Cabot made the first of two trips to the

Cabot Strait, a channel of water between Newfoundland and Cape Breton Island, was named after explorer John Cabot.

Newfoundland area on behalf of King Henry VII of England. Cabot reported that there were so many cod, he could scoop them up in baskets off the side of his ship. Historians are not certain whether Cabot and his crew actually landed in Newfoundland. Many European explorers followed Cabot, and the slow settlement of a "new founde lande" began.

Caravels were very fast ships that were useful for exploring new lands.

Gaspar Côrte-Real, a Portuguese explorer, spent the summer of 1500 exploring Newfoundland. He named many of the bays and inlets in the area. Côrte-Real and his crew sailed on caravels, a type of ship that was easy to maneuver.

The Norse who came to Newfoundland made the long voyage across the Atlantic between Europe and North America to bring back timber.

Cod fishing remained a staple industry into the 1800s and brought many immigrants to Newfoundland and Labrador.

EARLY SETTLERS

For almost a century after Cabot explored Newfoundland, fishers and whalers came to the province. Fishing boats from England, France, Spain, and Portugal arrived in Newfoundland waters. These fishers would haul in enormous catches of cod every summer. In 1583, despite the presence of fishing boats from many European countries, Sir Humphrey Gilbert claimed the Newfoundland territory for England.

Soon after Newfoundland was claimed, England's West Country Merchants were granted a **charter** that allowed them to establish colonies in Newfoundland. It also gave them exclusive rights to the area's offshore fishing grounds. The West Country Merchants did not want other permanent settlers in Newfoundland. They believed that settlers would compete with their profitable fishing fleets. The merchants went to great lengths to keep permanent settlers out.

The Spanish and Portuguese had fisheries in Newfoundland until the late 1600s.

Although Humphrey Gilbert did not create a permanent settlement in North America, he paved the way by claiming Newfoundland for England.

In 1610, an English merchant by the name of John Guy brought 39 settlers to Conception Bay. Guy and his settlers built a small community called Cupers Cove. By 1621, other settlements had been built at Cambriol, Renews, and Ferryland. These settlements were not successful. The harsh climate, poor soil, unprepared settlers, and threats from the West Country Merchants all contributed to the lack of success in settling.

Small settlements were established throughout the eighteenth century, but complaints about the brutality of the fishing **admirals** continued to reach Great Britain. In 1729, the British Crown appointed a naval officer to govern the island. This appointment brought some order to Newfoundland, and the settlement rate began to increase.

Once the territorial wars between Great Britain and other European countries came to an end, English and Irish settlers arrived more consistently. A great wave of immigration occurred during the early 1800s, when the British government made it legal for colonists to own land and build homes. By 1827, more than 60,000 people occupied Newfoundland.

Settlers started building lasting institutions, such as churches and government buildings, in the nineteenth century.

At the Castle Hill National Historic Site near Placentia, interpreters re-enact the fort's history in period clothing.

CULTURAL GROUPS

Newfoundland's citizens are mainly descendents of settlers from southwestern England, southern Ireland, and Scotland. About 96 percent of the population speaks English, and about 4 percent are bilingual, usually with French as the second language.

The province's people are different in many ways from other Canadians because they have been isolated for so long. One of the distinctive features is their manner of speaking. They have retained and modified the words and accents of their European ancestors. Many of the common words and phrases in Newfoundland are not so common in the rest of Canada. For example, Newfoundlanders call a small tin cup a "bannikin," a tourist is called a "come-from-away," and a pancake is called a "gandy."

Newfoundlanders are proud of their strong heritage and work hard to keep it alive. The Southern Newfoundland Seamen's Museum has exhibits of five centuries of sea-faring life at Grand Bank. Other sea-faring exhibits can be found throughout the province, and various historical sites preserve and explain Newfoundland's past.

The L'Anse aux Meadows National Historic Site reconstructs the Norse settlement on Newfoundland. It features displays of the Vikings' boats.

The custom of **mummering** is popular in Newfoundland. It dates back to early settlers. Mummers, who consist of both professional actors and everyday people, dress in costumes and perform traditional folk plays. They also parade through the streets. During the 12 days of Christmas, mummers go from house to house in their costumes and disguises. They try to fool their hosts who, in turn, must unmask their visitors by guessing their identity.

The Labrador Innu made eight different kinds of snowshoes.

Newfoundland's Aboriginal communities are also active in preserving and celebrating their cultures. A beach festival, held every July on Lake Melville, showcases aspects of Innu art and culture such as Innu tea dolls, hand-made moccasins, and wood and bone carvings. People at the festival also enjoy traditional Innu foods. The Labrador Inuit Association and the Torngâsok Cultural Centre work to protect Inuit language and culture for future generations. They help with education and give advice on understanding hunting regulations and land claims.

Mummers often make their costumes from materials they find in their homes.

Great Big Sea is part of Newfoundland's folk music tradition. They have been a band for 20 years.

ARTS AND ENTERTAINMENT

Newfoundland is far from the centres of mainstream Canadian music, art, and entertainment. As a result, most artists perform traditional songs, dances, and stories from the local area. More recently, new songs have been written about Newfoundland life and the sea. Newfoundland music often includes elements from Aboriginal music. Musicians play instruments that were played by their Scottish and Irish ancestors, such as the fiddle and the accordion.

The Newfoundland and Labrador **Folk Festival** has been held for **35 years.**

The Newfoundland music scene is gaining recognition outside the province. Professional performers, including Great Big Sea and Kim Stockwood, have become well known in Canada and the rest of the world. The annual Newfoundland and Labrador Folk Festival, at Bannerman Park in St. John's, attracts folk singers, musicians, and storytellers from Canada, the United States, and Europe. The festival helps preserve the cultural traditions of the province through music, dance, and crafts.

Gordon Pinsent has acted both on television and in movies. He currently lives in Toronto.

Newfoundland has also produced talented performers and writers. Rick Mercer, Mary Walsh, Cathy Jones, and Greg Thomey are all **Gemini Award** winners who have had success in television, radio, film, and writing. Nationally-known writer and commentator Rex Murphy was born just outside St. John's. Actor and writer Gordon Pinsent is from Grand Falls, Labrador, and has found great success with his Newfoundland stories.

Newfoundland books and theatre productions are often drawn from folklore and tradition. Some are based on the lonely life of the outposts, as in the works of novelists Margaret Daley, Wayne Johnston, and poet E.J. Pratt. Bernice Morgan was born in St. John's. She has written many award-winning novels, including *Random Passage*, which has sold more than 10,000 copies nation wide.

Wayne Johnston has written fiction, nonfiction, and short stories, many of which are related to Newfoundland.

SPORTS

Most of the athletics in Newfoundland and Labrador are at the amateur level and take advantage of the countryside, lakes, and sea. Many North Americans have enjoyed hunting in the woods and fishing on the bountiful waters of the province. Kayaking and canoeing are also popular water sports.

The majority of people in Labrador, and many on the island, own a snowmobile. Snowmobiling is a popular sport. It is also an excellent way of getting around when the land is frozen. The winter brings plenty of snowfall to the high land of Labrador and western Newfoundland. Downhill skiing, particularly at Marble Mountain near Corner Brook, is among the best in Canada. Labrador also offers ample opportunities for cross-country skiing.

People in Newfoundland and Labrador kayak for sport, sightseeing, and whale watching.

With more than 5,000 km of trails, snowmobile riders can enjoy Newfoundland and Labrador's pristine wilderness.

St. John's built many excellent sports facilities for the 1977 Canada Summer Games. For years, fans flocked to Newfoundland's Memorial Stadium to watch various sporting events, including the first-ever North American Ball Hockey Championships. In 2001, Mile One Centre replaced Memorial Stadium as the main venue for such events. The province has also hosted several gymnastic events.

The oldest sporting event in North America is the Royal St. John's Regatta. This 2.6-km, six-person rowing race has taken place on the first Wednesday of August since the 1820s. The carnival that accompanies the race is almost as important to the spectators as the race itself. Every year, more than 40,000 spectators attend the one-day Royal Regatta. The event is so popular that it is now an official municipal holiday. In 1901, a crew from Outer Cove set a race record for the Royal St. John's Royal Regatta that was unbeaten until 1981. The crew are in the Canadian Sports Hall of Fame.

The Mile One Centre is the home of the St. John's IceCaps, a hockey team in the American Hockey League.

How to Improve My Community

Strong communities make strong provinces. Think about what features are important in your community. What do you value? Education? Health? Forests? Safety? Beautiful spaces? Government works to help citizens create ideal living conditions that are fair to all by providing services in communities. Consider what changes you could make in your community. How would they improve your province as a whole? Using this concept web as a guide, write a report that outlines the features you think are most important in your community and what improvements could be made. A strong province needs strong communities.

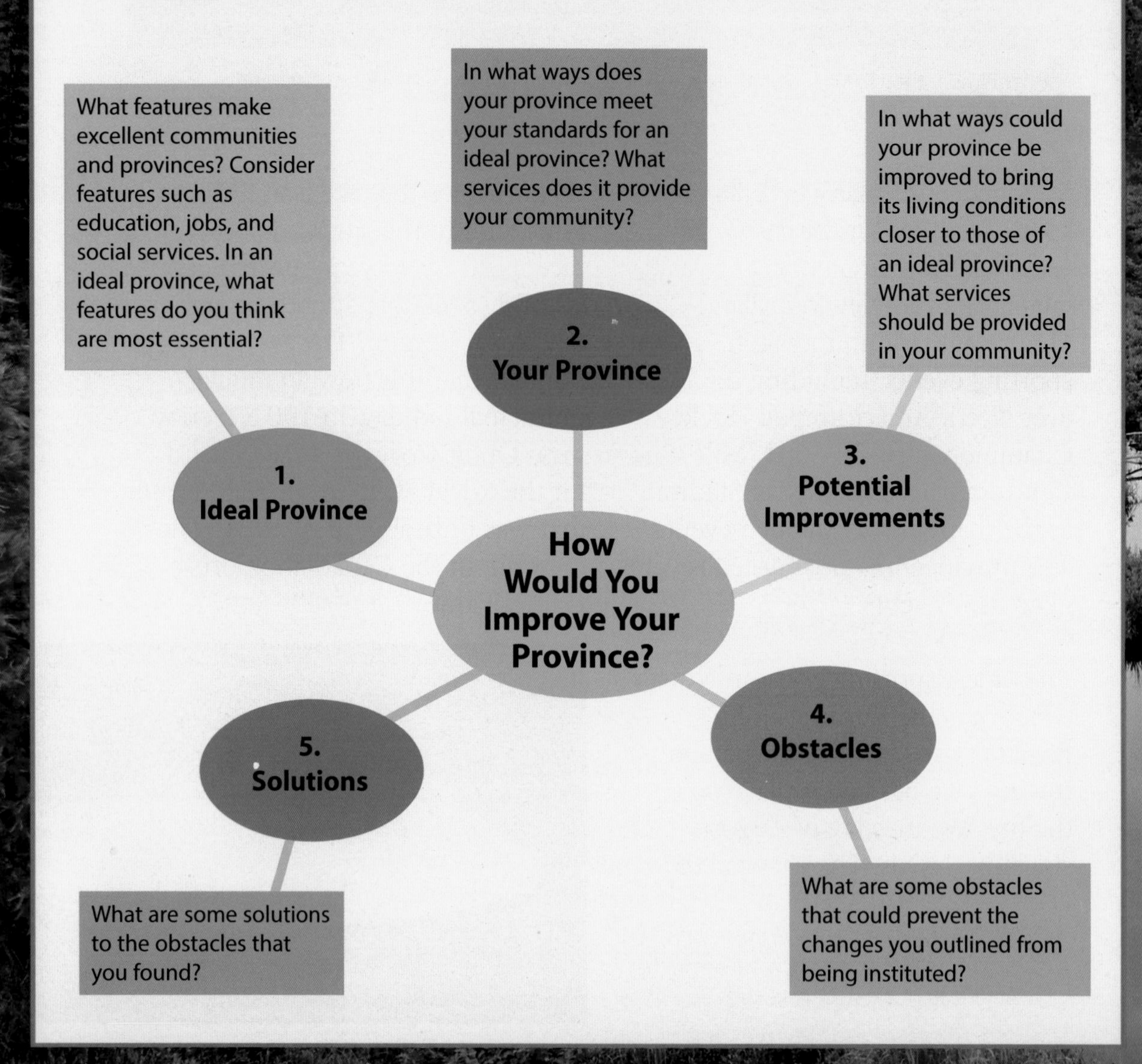

BRAIN TEASERS

Test your knowledge of Newfoundland and Labrador by trying to answer these brain teasers. The answers are printed upside down underneath each question.

1 What part of Newfoundland and Labrador is an island?

Newfoundland

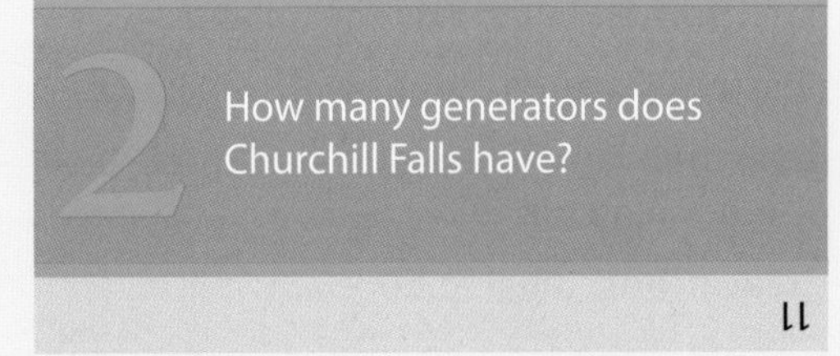

2 How many generators does Churchill Falls have?

11

3 In what year did Newfoundland become a province of Canada?

1949

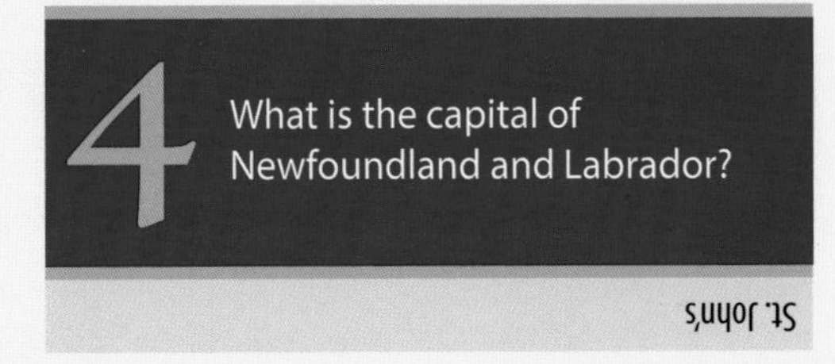

4 What is the capital of Newfoundland and Labrador?

St. John's

5 What is Newfoundland and Labrador's provincial bird?

Atlantic puffin

6 What Aboriginal group from Newfoundland first interacted with the Vikings?

The Beothuk

7 Who claimed the territory of Newfoundland for England?

Sir Humphrey Gilbert

8 What Newfoundland and Labrador sporting event is the oldest in North America?

Royal St. John's Regatta

Key Words

admirals: the leaders of fishing fleets

bogs: soft, wet areas of land

Canadian Shield: a region of ancient rock that encircles Hudson Bay and covers a large portion of Canada's mainland

charter: a written grant by a government

deposits: natural layers of sand, rock, coal, or other material

excavations: digging up

Gemini Award: an award that is given for excellence in Canadian television

hydro-electric: power produced by water power

mummering: a Newfoundland tradition that involves wearing a disguise and parading through the streets

Northwest Passage: a route for ships travelling from the Atlantic to the Pacific

plateau: level area of land

tundra: an Arctic or sub-arctic plain that remains frozen all year round

wigwams: dwellings that consist of cone-shaped frames covered with animal hides

Index